Picturesque
AMERICA

Picturesque AMERICA

Illustrations from the original 1874 edition, colored in the style of the period

The Mountains, Rivers, Lakes, Forests, Water-Falls, Shores, Canyons, Valleys, Cities, and other Picturesque Features of our Country by Eminent American Artists

Original preface by William Cullen Bryant
Preface to this edition by Oliver Jensen

American Heritage Publishing Co., Inc., New York
Book trade distribution by McGraw-Hill Book Company

Preface by Oliver Jensen copyright © 1974 by
Wolfe Publishing Limited
ISBN: 07-032461-1
Library of Congress Catalog Card No. 73-21908

Printed in Holland

Preface

There are as many Americas as there have been travellers to see them and hands to reproduce the scenes they have presented. For the motorist there are the endless throughways and interstates, smooth and neatly tended but paralyzing in their endless sameness, and for the air traveller the succession of cloud banks and toy landscapes miles below, interspersed with terminals stamped out each like the one before. The trickle of travellers who cling to the railroads see more, especially in the West, but they pass through nearly all the slums and workshops and junkyards of the land.

It is the traveller in history who perhaps sees the most of all, moving vicariously by foot or stagecoach or prairie schooner through time and experience. All he beholds is different, fresh prospects meeting his eye beyond every rise and river and range of mountains. His choice is broad among the artists who travelled the country almost from the first discoveries and settlement. He can marvel at John White's South, at Thomas Cole's Hudson, at Karl Bodmer's Plains, at Albert Bierstadt's Rockies. No European traveller with any talent at all forebore to record his impressions of the land, the towns, and the astonishing physiography of the New World, although the Americans themselves, busy with wresting a living from it, came late to recording it and especially to putting it in books. That stage in discovering America to ourselves waited until the nineteenth century and, of course, new processes in reproduction and printing.

With the opening of the West, curiosity about its wonders accelerated the process of self-discovery. The woodcut, taken from art and, beginning in the 1850's, from photographs, made it possible for the stay-at-home to be escorted down the rivers, across the prairies, and over the mountains. It took one through forest and canyon or to craggy peaks to look down on the plains below. The makers of newly popular city-views even lifted their customers high into the air for a somewhat prettified bird's-eye view of the works of man. All these are lost and haunting landscapes, and they are the business of this book.

Though long forgotten, the steel engravings reproduced here, hand colored from the originals, are classics of American illustration. They were the centerpieces of an enormous two-volume, leather-bound showpiece completed exactly a century ago under the title *Picturesque America*. In the florid style of the time the title ran on: *Or, The Land We Live in, A Delineation by Pen and Pencil of the Mountains, Rivers, Lakes, Forests, Water-Falls, Shores, Cañons, Valleys, Cities and other Picturesque Features of our Country, with Illustrations on Steel and Wood by Eminent American Artists.* And the books fulfilled their promise, from the coast of Maine to Florida and along the shores of the Pacific, crisscrossing the whole country in between, in over a thousand pages.

Teams of authors and artists were dispatched to do the country by "picturesque areas" ranging from whole states and rivers to more confined localities like Mount Desert Island or the Neversink Highlands. The authors are all forgotten today, their work of uneven quality; and the woodcuts, although sometimes excellent, cannot match the steel engravings, which were exactly as advertised, the work of eminent American artists in almost every case. They included many painters, noted then or later, like John F. Kensett, Worthington Whittredge, J. W. Casilear, Thomas Moran, and Homer Martin. And the project attracted many illustrators who had won fame covering the still-recent Civil War for magazines like *Harper's Weekly* and *Leslie's,* among them Alfred R. Waud, the English-born frontline artist with the Union armies, and William Ludlow Sheppard of Richmond, who had fought with and drawn the Confederate side. There was prolific Harry Fenn, a founder of the Society of Illustrators, who did more for *Picturesque America* than any other artist; and he was joined by J. D. Woodward, Granville Perkins, and F. O. C. Darley, all noted men in their time, landscapists par excellence, and A. C. Warren, who specialized in city views. It was a time when cities looked different each from the other, the time before cubelike skyscrapers, the time when a Providence or a Cincinnati or a St. Louis took pride in its character and uniqueness.

Is what we see in these pictures all romance? Was the Hudson so gleaming and placid, the Housatonic so pastoral, South Mountain so Gothic and its prospect so awe-inspiring? Were the Brooklyn gardens in the foreground so neat as one looks over them to Warren's view of New York? Was everyone so beautifully dressed and well-behaved? Aren't even the clouds a little overdressed? To ask the questions is to answer them. This is not rainy-day America, nor New York of the Bowery, but *picturesque* America, the wonders and achievements that an optimistic age wished to show as its face to the world. And in that sense it is realism heightened, distilled, and brought to life by art. There stand between the scene and our eyes, of course, not only the selectivity of the artist's mind and hand, but the skill of those nearly vanished craftsmen, the many steel engravers who took part in this project, artists in their own right, masters of shade and highlight who added drama to almost everything they touched. The engravings were purely black and white; neither color printing nor the halftone had been invented. It was the latter that made possible the printing of photographs and, by a kind of publishing Gresham's Law, drove out the steel engravers.

The man who brought *Picturesque America* together, whose own preface appears here, was the great poet and editor William Cullen Bryant. Born in 1794, he had been a poor country lawyer in Massachusetts, a pioneer in Illinois, and a magazine and newspaper editor in New York. A student of nature and crusader for freedom, he had raised the New York *Evening Post* to pre-eminence and was eighty, a patriarch in his sere and yellow leaf, when this project was completed. It was an eminently suitable task for the author of *A Forest Hymn, The Crowded Street,* and *Thanatopsis,* whose first lines run:

> To him who in the love of Nature holds
> Communion with her visible forms, she speaks
> A various language...

Oliver Jensen
Editor, *American Heritage*

From the Preface to the Original Edition, 1874

It is the design of the publication entitled *Picturesque America* to present full descriptions and elaborate pictorial delineations of the scenery characteristic of all the different parts of our country. The wealth of material for this purpose is almost boundless.

It will be admitted that our country abounds with scenery new to the artist's pencil, of a varied character, whether beautiful or grand, or formed of those sharper but no less striking combinations of outline which belong to neither of these classes. In the Old World every spot remarkable in these respects has been visited by the artist; studied and sketched again and again; observed in sunshine and in the shade of clouds, and regarded from every point of view that may give variety to the delineation. Both those who see in a landscape only what it shows to common eyes, and those whose imagination, like that of Turner, transfigures and glorifies whatever they look at, have made of these places, for the most part, all that could be made of them, until a desire is felt for the elements of natural beauty in new combinations, and for regions not yet rifled of all that they can yield to the pencil. Art sighs to carry her conquests into new realms. On our continent, and within the limits of our Republic, she finds them—primitive forests, in which the huge trunks of a past generation of trees lie mouldering in the shade of their aged descendants; mountains and valleys, gorges and rivers, and tracts of sea-coast, which the foot of the artist has never trod; and glens murmuring with water-falls which his ear has never heard. Thousands of charming nooks are waiting to yield their beauty to the pencil of the first comer. On the two great oceans which border our league of States, and in the vast space between them, we find a variety of scenery which no other single country can boast of. In other parts of the globe are a few mountains which attain a greater altitude than any within our limits, but the mere difference in height adds nothing to the impression made on the spectator. Among our White Mountains, our Catskills, our Alleghanies, our Rocky Mountains, and our Sierra Nevada, we have some of the wildest and most beautiful scenery in the world. On our majestic rivers—among the largest on either continent—and on our lakes—the largest and noblest in the world—the country often wears an aspect in which beauty is blended with majesty; and on our prairies and savannas the spectator, surprised at the vastness of their features, finds himself, notwithstanding the soft and gentle sweep of their outlines, overpowered with a sense of sublimity.

By means of the overland communications lately opened between the Atlantic coast and that of the Pacific, we have now easy access to scenery of a most remarkable character. For those who would see Nature in her grandest forms of snow-clad mountain, deep valley, rocky pinnacle, precipice, and chasm, there is no longer any occasion to cross the ocean. A rapid journey by railway over the plains that stretch westward from the Mississippi, brings the tourist into a region of the Rocky Mountains rivalling Switzerland in its scenery of rock piled on rock, up to the region of the clouds. But Switzerland has no such groves on its mountain-sides, nor has even Libanus, with its ancient cedars, as those which raise the astonishment of the visitor to that Western region—trees of such prodigious height and enormous dimensions that, to attain their present bulk, we might imagine them to have sprouted from the seed at the time of the Trojan War. Another feature of that region is so remarkable as to have enriched our language with a new word; and *cañon*, as the Spaniards write it, or *canyon*, as it is often spelled by our people, signifies one of those chasms between perpendicular walls of rock—chasms of fearful depth and of length like that of a river, reporting of some mighty convulsion of Nature in ages that have left no record save in these displacements of the crust of our globe. Nor should we overlook in this enumeration the scenery of the desert, as it is seen in all its dreariness, not without offering subjects for the pencil, in those tracts of our Western possessions where rains never fall nor springs gush to moisten the soil.

When we speak of the scenery in our country rivalling that of Switzerland, we do not mean to imply that it has not a distinct and peculiar aspect. In mountain-scenery Nature does not repeat herself any more than in the human countenance. The traveller among the Pyrenees sees at a glance that he is not among the Alps. There is something in the forms and tints by which he is surrounded, and even in the lights which fall upon them, that impresses him with the idea of an essential difference. So, when he journeys among the steeps, and gorges, and fountains of Lebanon and Anti-Lebanon, he well perceives that he is neither among the Alps nor the Pyrenees. The precipices wear outlines of their own, the soil has its peculiar vegetation, the clouds and the sky have their distinct physiognomy.

Here, then, is a field for the artist almost without limits. It is no wonder that, with such an abundance and diversity of subjects for the pencil of the landscape-painter, his art should flourish in our country, and that some of those by whom it is practised should have made themselves illustrious by their works. Amid this great variety, however, and in a territory of such great extent, parts of which are but newly explored and other parts yet unvisited by sketchers, it is certain that no country has within its borders so many beautiful spots altogether unfamiliar to its own people. It is quite safe to assert that a book of American scenery, like *Picturesque America,* will lay before American readers more scenes entirely new to them than a similar book on Europe. Paintings, engravings, and photographs, have made us all, even those who have never seen them, well acquainted with the banks of the Hudson, with Niagara, and with the wonderful valley of the Yosemite; but there are innumerable places which lie out of the usual path of our artists and tourists; and many strange, picturesque, and charming scenes, sought out in these secluded spots, will, for the first time, become familiar to the general public through these pages. It is the purpose of the work to illustrate with greater fullness, and with superior excellence, so far as art is concerned, the places which attract curiosity by their interesting associations, and, at the same time, to challenge the admiration of the public for many of the glorious scenes which lie in the by-ways of travel....

William Cullen Bryant

List of Engravings

From Volume One

Subject	Artist	Engraver
Cascade in Virginia *(title page)*	Harry Fenn	*R. Hinshelwood*
Niagara	Harry Fenn	*S. V. Hunt*
Mount Desert, Coast of Maine	Harry Fenn	*R. Hinshelwood*
On the Coast of Florida	Harry Fenn	*R. Hinshelwood*
Mount Hood, from the Columbia River	R. Swain Gifford	*R. Hinshelwood*
Richmond, from the James	Harry Fenn	*R. Hinshelwood*
Delaware Water Gap	Granville Perkins	*R. Hinshelwood*
Smoky Mountains, North Carolina	Homer Martin	*R. Hinshelwood*
Mount Washington Road	Harry Fenn	*S. V. Hunt*
The Highlands of the Neversink	Granville Perkins	*W. Wellstood*
Cumberland Gap	Harry Fenn	*S. V. Hunt*
City of New Orleans	Alfred R. Waud	*D. G. Thompson*
Upper Falls of the Yellowstone	Thomas Moran	*S. V. Hunt*
Harper's Ferry, by Moonlight	Granville Perkins	*R. Hinshelwood*
The Chickahominy	W. L. Sheppard	*W. Wellstood*
Baptism Bay, Lake Superior	William Hart	*R. Hinshelwood*
Mount Shasta	James D. Smillie	*E. P. Brandard*
Mirror Lake, Yosemite Valley	Harry Fenn	*S. V. Hunt*
City of Providence	A. C. Warren	*R. Hinshelwood*
Indian Rock, Narragansett	Wm. S. Haseltine	*S. V. Hunt*
City of Buffalo	A. C. Warren	*W. Wellstood*
City of Cleveland	A. C. Warren	*R. Hinshelwood*
City of Detroit	A. C. Warren	*R. Hinshelwood*
The Golden Gate	James D. Smillie	*E. P. Brandard*

From Volume Two

Subject	Artist	Engraver
Dome of the Capitol *(title page)*	Harry Fenn	*E. P. Brandard*
New York, from Brooklyn Heights	A. C. Warren	*G. R. Hall*
West Point	Harry Fenn	*S. V. Hunt*
Mouth of the Moodna	David Johnson	*G. W. Wellstood*
Philadelphia, from Belmont	Granville Perkins	*R. Hinshelwood*
Connecticut Valley, from Mount Tom	J. D. Woodward	*S. V. Hunt*
Baltimore, from Druid Hill Park	Granville Perkins	*R. Hinshelwood*
Sunrise, from South Mountain, the Catskills	Harry Fenn	*S. V. Hunt*
City of Cincinnati	A. C. Warren	*W. Wellstood*
City of Louisville	A. C. Warren	*E. P. Brandard*
Emigrants Crossing the Plains	F. O. C. Darley	*H. B. Hall*
Californians Lassoing Bear	F. O. C. Darley	*F. Holl*
The Susquehanna	Granville Perkins	*R. Hinshelwood*
Boston, from South Boston	J. D. Woodward	*E. P Brandard*
Lake George	J. W. Casilear	*R. Hinshelwood*
The Housatonic	A. F. Bellows	*S. V. Hunt*
The City of St. Louis	A. C. Warren	*R. Hinshelwood*
Quebec	J. D. Woodward	*R. Hinshelwood*
Beverly Coast, Massachusetts	J. F. Kensett	*S. V. Hunt*
Adirondack Woods	J. M. Hart	*R. Hinshelwood*
East Rock, New Haven	C. G. Griswold	*S. V. Hunt*
The Rocky Mountains	W. Whittredge	*R. Hinshelwood*
City of Milwaukee	A. C. Warren	*R. Hinshelwood*
Terrace, Central Park	C. Rosenberg	*G. R. Hall*
Washington, from Arlington Heights	W. L. Sheppard	*R. Hinshelwood*

Volume One

Harry Fenn

Entered according to Act of Congress, AD 1873, in the Office of the Librarian of Congress, Washington

S.V. Hunt

Mount Desert, Coast of Maine

Harry Fenn

Entered according to Act of Congress, AD 1871, in the Office of the Librarian of Congress, Washington

R. Hinshelwood

On the Coast of Florida

R.S. Gifford

R. Hinshelwood

Mount Hood from the Columbia

Richmond from the James

G. Perkins   *Entered according to Act of Congress, AD 1872, in the Office of the Librarian of Congress, Washington*   R. Hinshelwood

Delaware Water Gap

Homer Martin

Entered according to Act of Congress, AD 1873, in the Office of the Librarian of Congress, Washington

R. Hinshelwood

The Smoky Mountains

NORTH CAROLINA

The Mount Washington Road

WHITE MOUNTAINS

Granville Perkins

W. Wellstood

The Highlands of the Neversink

H. Fenn

Entered according to Act of Congress, AD 1872, in the Office of the Librarian of Congress, Washington

S.V. Hunt

Cumberland Gap

A.R. Waud   *Entered according to Act of Congress, AD 1873, in the Office of the Librarian of Congress, Washington*   D.G. Thompson

The Upper Yellowstone Falls

G. Perkins   *Entered according to Act of Congress, AD 1874, in the Office of the Librarian of Congress, Washington*   R. Hinshelwood

Harper's Ferry by Moonlight

W. L. Sheppard

Entered according to Act of Congress, AD 1872, in the Office of the Librarian of Congress, Washington

W. Wellstood

The Chickahominy

William Hart

Entered according to Act of Congress, AD 1873, in the Office of the Librarian of Congress, Washington

R. Hinshelwood

ENTRANCE TO BAPTISM BAY

Lake Superior

ENTRANCE TO BAPTISM BAY

Mount Shasta

Harry Fenn   *Entered according to Act of Congress, AD 1872, in the Office of the Librarian of Congress, Washington*   S.V. Hunt

Mirror Lake, Yosemite Valley

A.C. Warren

Entered according to Act of Congress, AD 1872, in the Office of the Librarian of Congress, Washington

R. Hinshelwood

City of Providence

FROM PROSPECT HILL

Indian Rock

NARRAGANSETT

A.C. Warren

W. Wellstood

City of Buffalo

A.C. Warren

Entered according to Act of Congress, AD 1872, in the Office of the Librarian of Congress, Washington

R. Hinshelwood

City of Cleveland

FROM RESERVOIR WALK

The City of Detroit

FROM CANADA SHORE

Golden Gate

FROM TELEGRAPH HILL

Volume Two

A.C. Warren

Entered according to Act of Congress, AD 1872, in the Office of the Librarian of Congress, Washington

G.R. Hall

City of New York

FROM BROOKLYN HEIGHTS

H. Fenn

Entered according to Act of Congress, AD 1869, in the clerk's office of the district court of the southern district of New York

S.V. Hunt

West Point and the Highlands

David Johnson

G.W. Wellstood

Mouth of the Moodna, on the Hudson

G. Perkins

Entered according to Act of Congress, AD 1873, in the Office of the Librarian of Congress, Washington

R. Hinshelwood

Philadelphia from Belmont

WEST PARK

J.D. Woodward

S.V. Hunt

Connecticut Valley from Mount Tom

G. Perkins

R. Hinshelwood

City of Baltimore

FROM DRUID HILL PARK

Harry Fenn   *Entered according to Act of Congress, A.D. 1873, in the Office of the Librarian of Congress, Washington*   S. V. Hunt

The Catskills

SUNRISE FROM SOUTH MOUNTAIN

City of Cincinnati

A.C. Warren

Entered according to Act of Congress, AD 1872, in the Office of the Librarian of Congress, Washington

E.P. Brandard

City of Louisville

F.O.C. Darley

Entered according to Act of Congress, AD 1869, in the clerk's office of the district court for the southern district of New York

H.B. Hall

Emigrants Crossing the Plains

F.O.C. Darley

Entered according to Act of Congress in the year 1873 in the Office of the Librarian of Congress at Washington

Francis Holl

Native Californians Lassoing a Bear

The Susquehanna

AT HUNTER'S GAP

City of Boston

FROM SOUTH BOSTON

J.W. Casilear

R. Hinshelwood

Lake George

FROM A PAINTING BY A. F. BELLOWS

A.C. Warren

R. Hinshelwood

City of St. Louis

Quebec

On the Beverly Coast, Massachusetts

FROM A PAINTING BY J. F. KENSETT

The Adirondack Woods

FROM A PAINTING BY J. M. HART

C.G. Griswold

Entered according to Act of Congress, AD 1873, in the Office of the Librarian of Congress, Washington

S.V. Hunt

East Rock, New Haven

W. Whittredge

R. Hinshelwood

The Rocky Mountains

A.C. Warren
Entered according to Act of Congress, AD 1872, in the Office of the Librarian of Congress, Washington
R. Hinshelwood

City of Milwaukee

The Terrace, Central Park

NEW YORK

Washington from Arlington Heights